BATS IN THE DARK

Doreen Gonzales

PowerKiDS press.

New York

Published in 2010 by The Rosen Publishing Group, Inc.
29 East 21st Street, New York, NY 10010

First Edition

Editor: Amelie von Zumbusch
Book Design: Julio Gil
Photo Researcher: Jessica Gerweck

Photo Credits: Cover Bob Elsdale/Getty Images; pp. 5, 13 © Joe McDonald/Corbis; p. 6 © Gary Braasch/Corbis; p. 9 James Hager/Getty Images; p. 10 Shutterstock.com; p. 14 © Frans Lanting/Corbis; p. 17 Tim Laman/Getty Images; p. 18 Win-Initiative/Getty Images; p. 21 John Cancalosi/age fotostock.

Library of Congress Cataloging-in-Publication Data

Gonzales, Doreen.
  Bats in the dark / Doreen Gonzales. — 1st ed.
      p. cm. — (Creatures of the night)
  Includes index.
  ISBN 978-1-4042-8096-0 (library binding) — ISBN 978-1-4358-3249-7 (pbk.) —
ISBN 978-1-4358-3250-3 (6-pack)
  1. Bats—Juvenile literature. I. Title.
  QL737.C5G635 2010
  599.4—dc22
                                        2008053802

Manufactured in the United States of America

Contents

A Flying Mammal

Imagine spending your days hanging upside down. This is what bats do. Bats are **nocturnal** animals that fly around at night looking for food. At sunrise, they return to their homes to hang upside down and sleep. Bats are the only **mammals** that fly. They have small bodies and long, wide wings.

A nocturnal life is good for bats. Many kinds of bats eat **insects** that fly around at night. Night feeding also keeps bats safe from animals that might eat them. Though flying is hard work, the cool night air keeps bats' bodies from getting too hot.

As many mammals do, bats often have furry bodies. You can see the fur on this pallid bat. Pallid bats live in the dry parts of western North America.

Mega or Micro?

There are about 1,000 different kinds of bats. **Scientists** put bats into two groups. These groups are the megabats and the microbats. All microbats are less than 6 inches (15 cm) long. The smallest is only 1 inch (2.5 cm) long. Microbats use their hearing to find food in the darkness.

"Mega" means "huge." Though a few megabats are small, many of these mammals are large. For example, flying foxes have wings that are as wide as 6 feet (2 m) from tip to tip! All megabats use sight and smell to find food. Their large eyes help them see at night.

"Micro" means "small," but some microbats are huge. American false vampire bats, such as this one, can be between 2 and 3 feet (61–91 cm) from wing tip to wing tip.

Bat Wings

Every bat's body is small compared to its wings. Bats are covered in brown, black, gray, yellow, or red fur. A bat's wings are formed by bones that look like long fingers. Thin skin covers these bones. Bats can change the shape of their wings by moving their wing bones around. This lets them quickly change direction as they fly through the night sky.

Bats have a claw that sticks out of each wing. They use this claw to climb. Bats' toes also have claws that help them hold on to things.

Bat wings are strong and bend very easily. If a bat tears its wing, the wing will heal quickly. This is important because bats must fly to find food.

Just Hanging Around

Bats live on every **continent** except Antarctica. Some bats live in **rain forests**, while others live in deserts. Wherever they live, bats roost in dark, out-of-the-way places during the day. Bats like to roost in caves, rocky places, and trees. They also live under bridges and in barns.

When bats find somewhere safe to roost, they take hold with their claws and hang with their heads pointing down. Then, they fold their wings around their bodies and go to sleep. Bats sleep upside down because they cannot take off flying from the ground. They must fall into flight.

These flying foxes are sleeping in a tree in Sydney, Australia. During the day, it is common to see these bats resting in Sydney's Royal Botanic Gardens.

What's for Dinner?

Many megabats eat fruit, while others feed on flowers. Most microbats are **insectivores**. These bats eat insects, such as moths and crickets. Bats catch small insects in their mouths. Bats catch large insects with a wing and then pull them into their mouths. Bats can eat as many as 1,000 insects every hour!

Some microbats eat small animals, such as birds, lizards, and frogs. As you might guess, fish-eating bats eat mostly fish. Vampire bats eat the most surprising food. These bats bite animals and lick the blood from the bite. Vampire bats feed on cows, horses, and deer.

This hungry little brown bat is eating a katydid. Little brown bats also eat beetles, moths, and mosquitoes.

HUNTING WITH SOUND

Many bats can see well. However, because they hunt at night, it is too dark to see much. Therefore, they also use other methods to find their dinner. For example, megabats use smell along with sight to find food.

Microbats hunt with sound. They make beeping noises as they fly. They listen for a beep to **echo** off of something in their path. Bats use this echo to figure out where an object, such as a tasty insect, is. The echo also tells the bat how large the object is, which direction it is moving, and how fast it is moving. This method of finding food is called echolocation.

Fishing bats, such as this one, use echolocation to sense tiny waves made by underwater fish. The bats then dive down and pull the fish out of the water.

Life as a Bat

Some bats live alone. Others live in groups, called colonies. Bat colonies can have thousands of bats. Bats in colonies take care of each other and even bring food to bats that are sick.

Bats that live where the weather gets cold cannot find food in the winter. Many of these bats **hibernate**. Hibernating bats find a roost and hang. In time, their bodies cool down and their breathing slows. By hibernating, bats can live through times when there is little food. Other bats from cold places **migrate** to warm places when winter comes. The bats return home in the spring.

Wrinkle-lipped bats live in caves across Southeast Asia. They often live in colonies that have hundreds of thousands of bats!

PUPS

Most bats have only one baby at a time. A baby bat is called a pup. Pups drink their mothers' milk. Mother bats sometimes carry their new pups with them when they go out to feed. More often, mothers leave their pups at the roost. Mother bats return to feed their babies several times during the night. Sometimes pups are cared for by others in the colony.

Bat babies are about a quarter of their mothers' size. For most mammals, the difference between adults and babies is much bigger. Bat pups grow quickly, too. Many kinds of bat pups can fly about three weeks after they are born. Bats can live for 20 years or more.

Since they cannot fly, bat pups hang on to their mothers most of the time. Newborn bats have strong claws and legs.

BAT TALES

Some people believe bats are a sign of luck or happiness. Other people tell scary stories about bats. One story tells of bats turning into vampires at night. Vampires are monsters who suck people's blood in stories. Though people know vampires are not real, some people are still afraid of bats.

People sometimes worry that bats will fly into their hair. Others fear a bat will bite them and give them **rabies**. However, bats generally stay away from people and do not often bite them. Bats do sometimes carry rabies, though, so they should be handled carefully.

Some people become scared or nervous when the sky is full of bats. Others love to watch these interesting nocturnal animals.

WE NEED BATS

Bats are among Earth's most interesting and helpful animals. Some kinds of bats eat bugs that can make people sick and insects that destroy crops. Other types of bats help plants by spreading their seeds.

Today, though, bats are in danger. People keep moving into places where bats live. This leaves the bats without a home. Several kinds of bats, such as the bumblebee bat, the Mariana flying fox, and the Ozark big-eared bat, are even in danger of dying out. Luckily, people have started finding ways to keep bats and their homes safe. If we work together, bats will fill the night skies for many years to come!

Glossary

CONTINENT (KON-tuh-nent) One of Earth's seven large landmasses.

ECHO (EH-koh) To hear a sound again when it is thrown back by an object.

HIBERNATE (HY-bur-nayt) To spend the winter in a sleeplike state.

INSECTIVORES (in-SEK-tih-vorz) Animals that eat insects for food.

INSECTS (IN-sekts) Small animals that often have six legs and wings.

MAMMALS (MA-mulz) Warm-blooded animals that have backbones and hair, breathe air, and feed milk to their young.

MIGRATE (MY-grayt) To move from one place to another.

NOCTURNAL (nok-TUR-nul) Active during the night.

RABIES (RAY-beez) A deadly illness that wild animals can carry.

RAIN FORESTS (RAYN FOR-ests) Thick forests that receive large amounts of rain during the year.

SCIENTISTS (SY-un-tists) People who study the world.

INDEX

WEB SITES

Due to the changing nature of Internet links, PowerKids Press has developed an online list of Web sites related to the subject of this book. This site is updated regularly. Please use this link to access the list: www.powerkidslinks.com/cnight/bat/